I Can See

by Rachel Vazquez

HOUGHTON MIFFLIN BOSTON

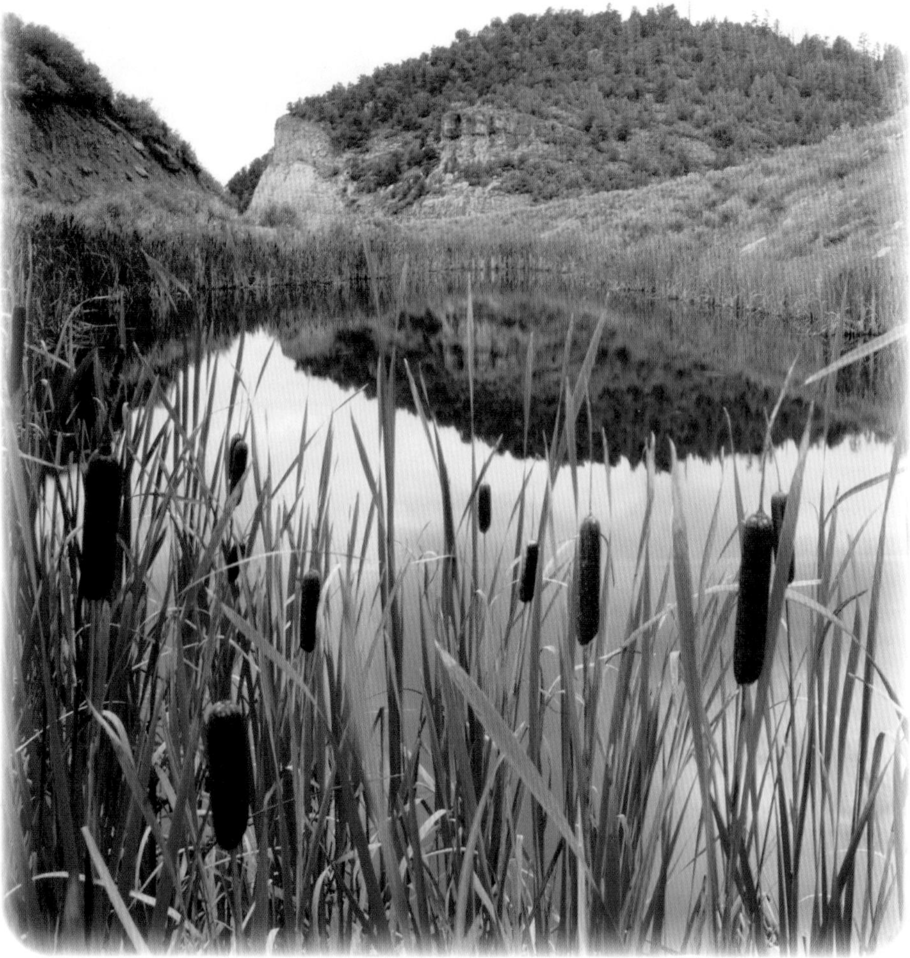

I can see a pond.

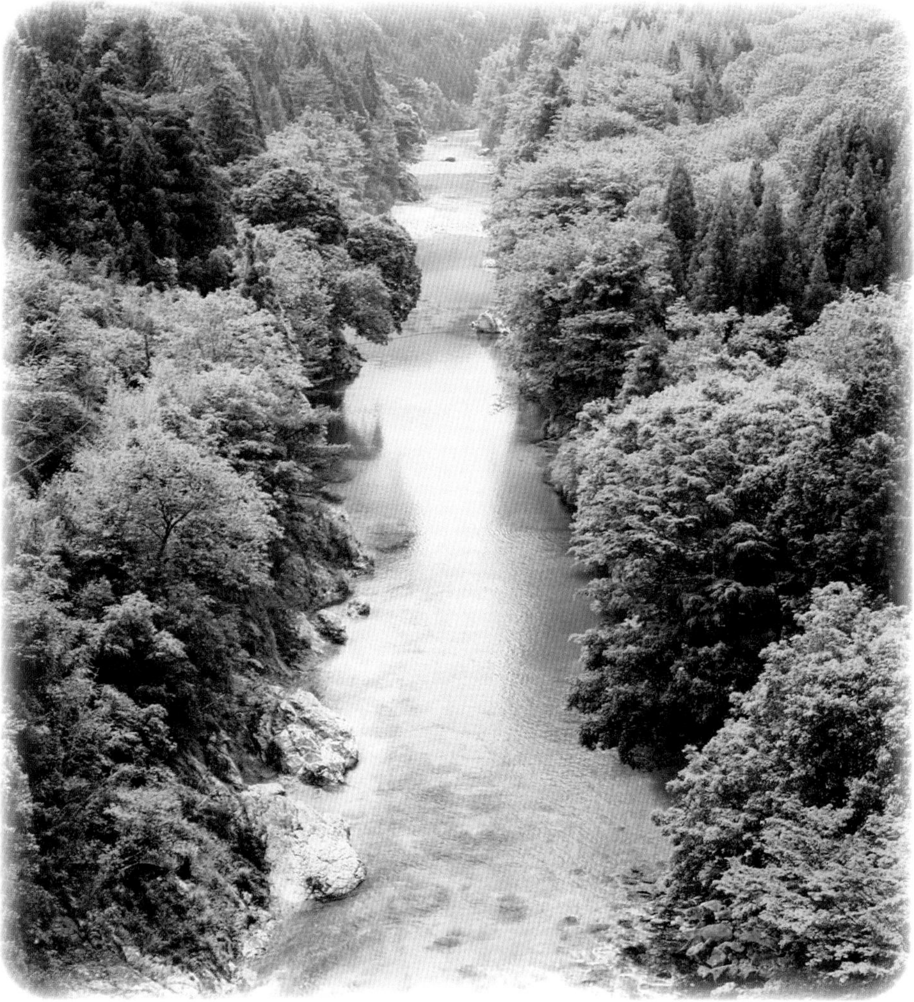

I can see a river.

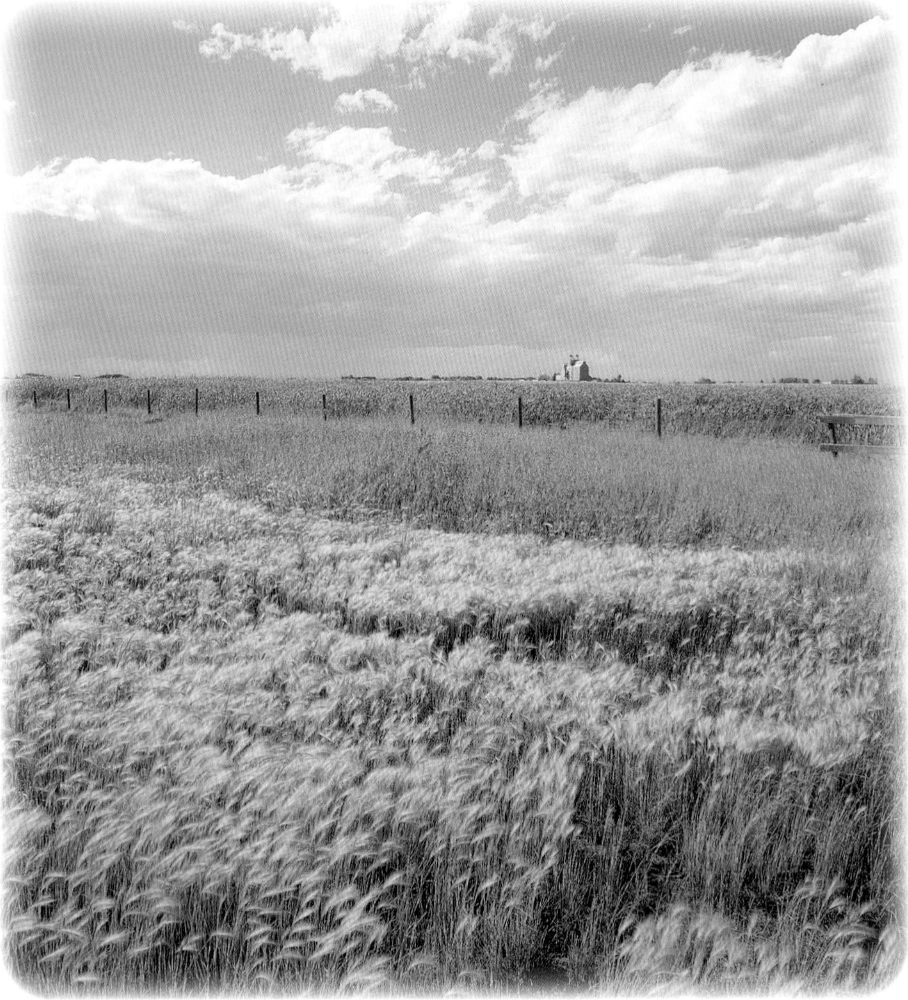

I can see a field.

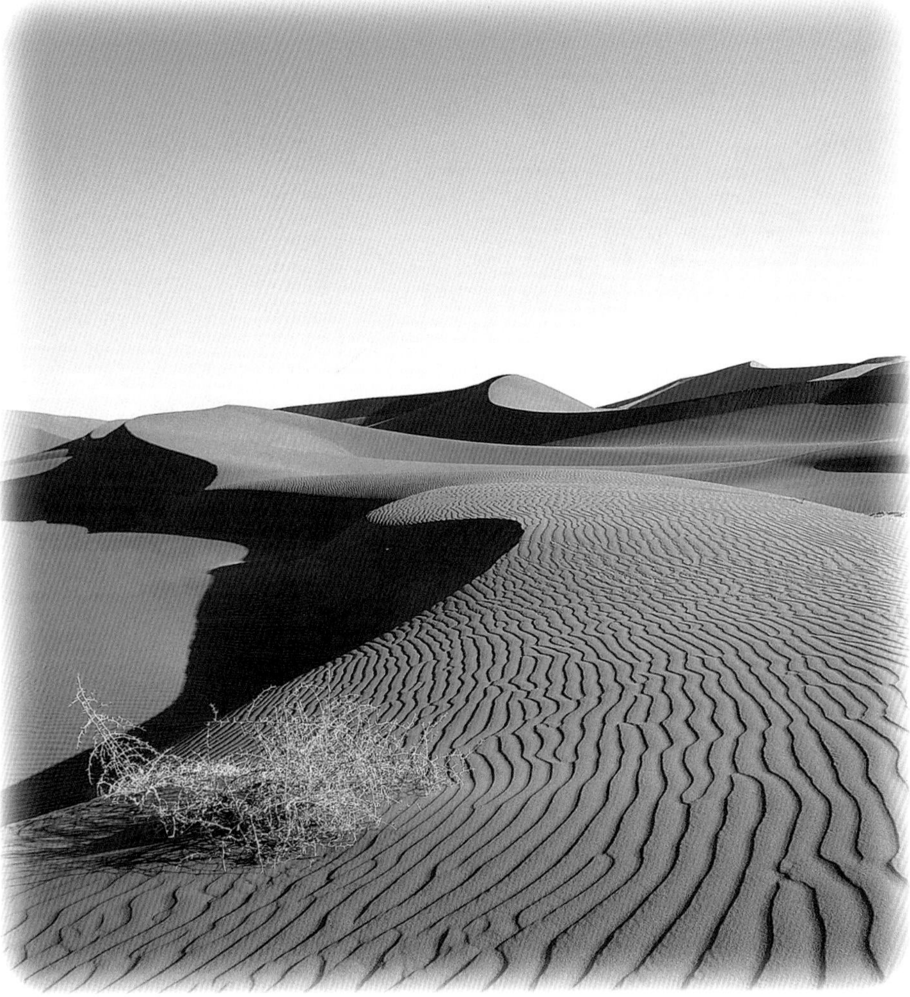

I can see a desert.

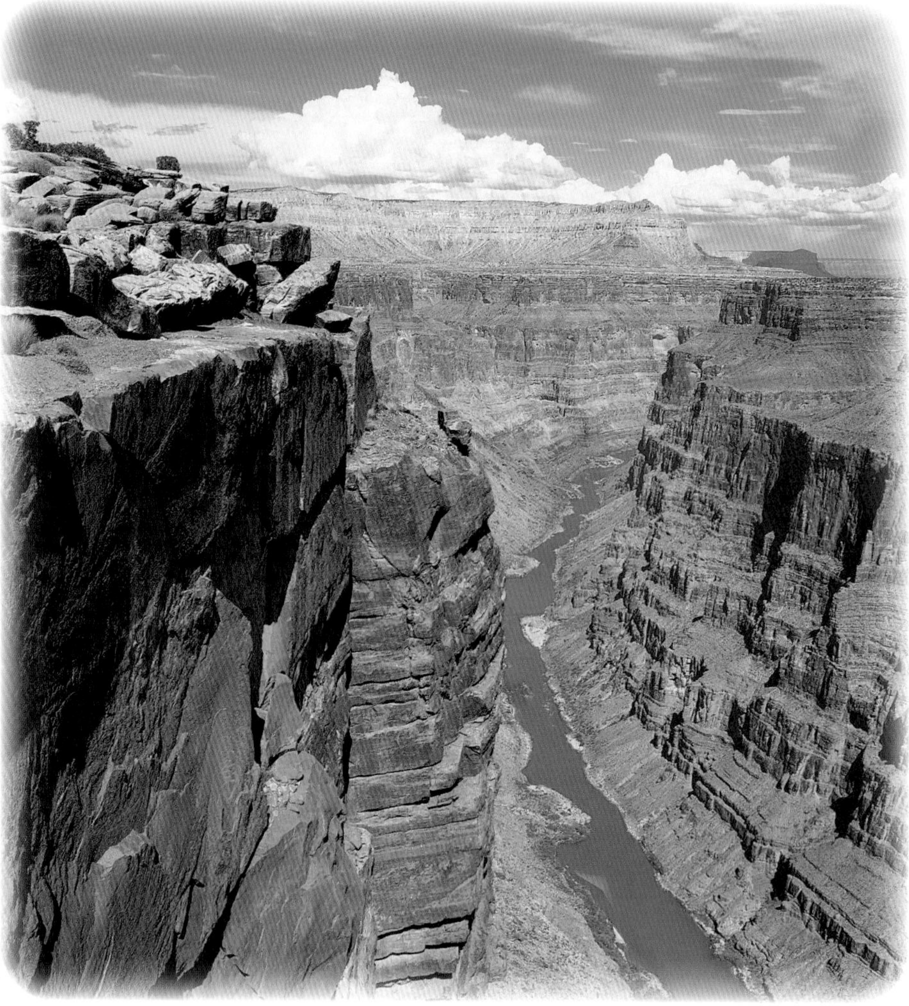

I can see a canyon.

I can see a hill.

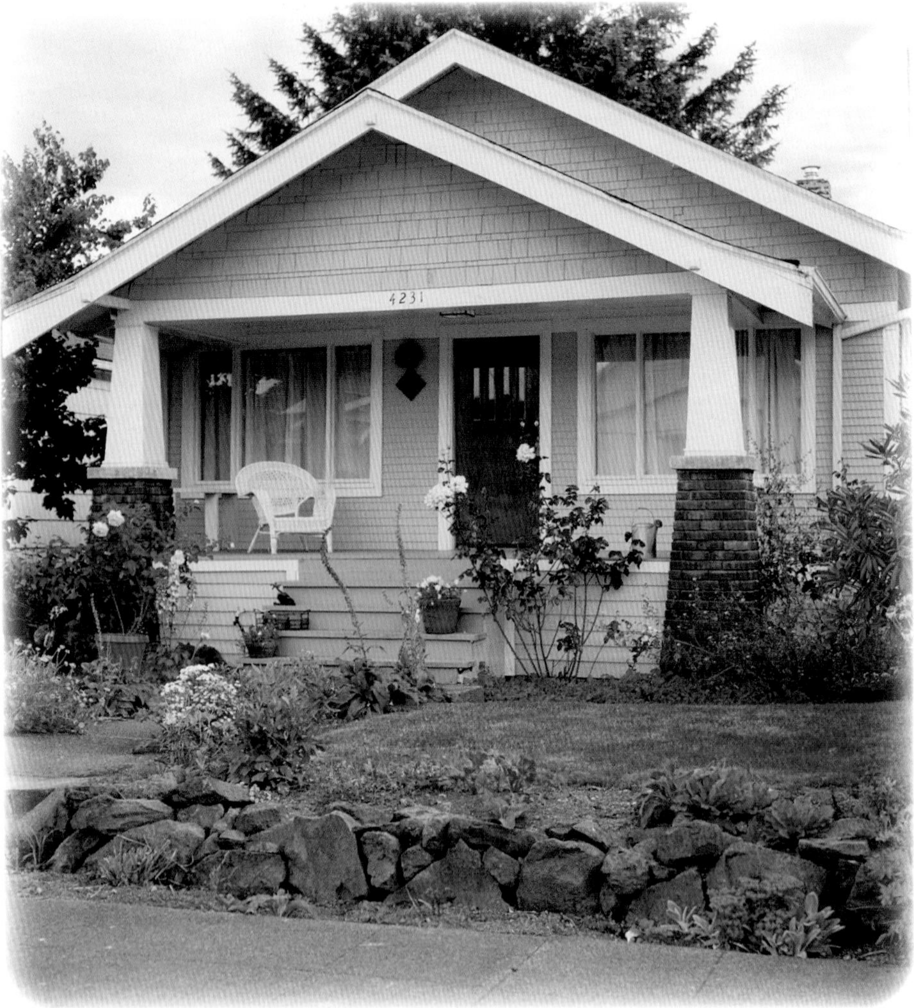

I can see my home.